DATE DUE

MORE THAN A HERO

MORE THAN A HERO

MUHAMMAD ALI'S LIFE LESSONS
PRESENTED THROUGH HIS DAUGHTER'S EYES

HANA ALI

POCKET BOOKS

NEW YORK   LONDON   TORONTO   SYDNEY   SINGAPORE

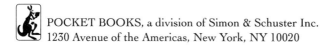 POCKET BOOKS, a division of Simon & Schuster Inc.
1230 Avenue of the Americas, New York, NY 10020

Library of Congress Cataloging-in-Publication Data

Ali, Muhammad, 1942–
   More than a hero : Muhammad Ali's life lessons presented through
   his daughter's eyes / Hana Ali.
     p. cm.
   ISBN 0-671-04236-X
    1. Ali, Muhammad, 1942– 2. Boxers (Sports)—United States—Biography.
    3. Ali, Hana.
  I. Ali, Hana. II. Title.

GV1132.A44 A34 2000
796.83'092—dc21
[B]   00-027422

First Pocket Books hardcover printing May 2000

10 9 8 7 6 5 4 3 2 1

This book is dedicated to my father
and all the other philanthropists of the world.
You have taken a piece from the puzzle of life
and embedded it in its rightful place.
You share a confluence of love and light
that few people have had the honor of witnessing firsthand.
Continue to prevail on your journey.
Never give up hope.
Never let your heart skip a beat.
And most important, never stop loving, because the world can never
have too many open hearts—
and we can never have enough people working together
to make a difference.

For Timothy, may the sunlight always find you.

Hana Yasmeen Ali

BUTTERFLY

Float like a butterfly.
Sting like a bee.
Your hands can't hit
what your eyes can't see.

—Muhammad Ali

INTRODUCTION

T H E   W O R L D knows my father as Muhammad Ali, né Cassius Clay, a man with one of the most recognized faces on the planet. I know him as Daddy.

When I was a young girl, no more than nine or ten years old, I remember the first time I saw my father after he and my mother separated. Beforehand I was so excited that I could hardly wait to get where he and Lonnie, his current wife, were staying at the Disneyland Hotel, in Anaheim, California.

If memory serves me correctly, I was wearing a little white tank top and a short black skirt. I had been raised Orthodox Muslim, so I had never before worn such revealing clothing while in my father's presence. When we finally arrived, the chauffeur escorted my younger sister, Laila, and me up to my father's suite. As usual, he was hiding behind the door waiting to scare us. We exchanged as many hugs and kisses as we could possibly give in one day. My father took a good look at us. Then, he sat me down on his lap and said something that I will never forget. He looked me straight in the eyes and said, "Hana, everything that God made valuable in the world is covered and hard to get to. Where do you find diamonds? Deep down in the ground, covered and protected. Where do you find pearls? Deep down at the bottom of the ocean, covered up and protected in a beautiful shell. Where do you find gold? Way down in the mine, covered over with layers and layers of rock. You've got to work hard to get to them." He looked at me with serious eyes. "Your body is sacred. You're far more precious than diamonds and pearls, and you should be covered too."

This is just one of the many lessons that my father instilled and continues to instill in me and my sisters, then and now. This book of poetry and memories was inspired by these recollections and by my father's poems written in his earlier years. Another thing that inspired me to put this book together was my father's uninhibited love for people. I don't think people know just how big his heart truly is.

One of my fondest memories of the house I grew up in was of coming home after elementary school. I'd run straight into my father's office and jump onto his lap, giving him bunches of hugs and kisses. After a few hours of drawing or coloring pictures on the office floor by the fireplace, I would head upstairs to my room to play some more. Once, when I was seven, I found a strange person in my bed. I ran right down to my dad and rambled on about how burglars had broken into the house and they were in my room snoring loudly! He calmed me down and explained that the people I saw were not burglars. They were a homeless family that had no place to live and no food to eat.

My father was, and still is, always doing great things like that. One time, he got a telephone call about a young man who was threatening to jump off of a building a few blocks away from our house.

The man was a Vietnam veteran who felt he had nothing left to live for. My father immediately dropped what he was doing, drove to the location, got out on the ledge with the young man, and talked him back inside the window. Soon thereafter, my father found him an apartment and paid the rent until the vet could find a decent job.

Yes, my father is a hero! The world knows it, and I know it. However, I get the privilege of witnessing the little things, which in the end are really where true heroism lies. For example, I once asked my father how he finds the strength to do all that he does. He gracefully replied, "Service to others is the rent we pay for our room here on earth." Not too long after that conversation, Lonnie, Laila, Asaad (who is the youngest of us all), my father, and I were driving to his home from the airport in the rain around eleven-thirty at night. A big bus of tourists recognized my dad in the passenger seat. My father asked Lonnie to pull over. He signed autographs and took pictures with every soul on that bus! I clearly recall thinking, *I understand him.* I know how truly blessed I am to be able to be with an angel that is my daddy.

On one occasion we almost missed our flight back to Chicago out of New York City. Dad was signing autographs. By the time we boarded the plane, a man and his son from coach were sitting in our first-class seats.

When the flight attendant asked them to resume their original seats, my father stopped her and asked the little boy if he had ever flown first class. The boy shyly replied, "No." My dad smiled and said, "Then this is your lucky day." The boy's father thanked us, and we headed to the back of the plane to our new seats. As you can see, my father passed a hero's test far beyond all the best.

My father and I collaborated on this project. It contains both his poetry and several of my own poems dedicated to him, as well as other heartwarming stories about him. The collection reveals Muhammad Ali's true heart, nature, and moral beliefs. I hope you will enjoy these special recollections and glimpses into the world of my father as much as we enjoyed living those times.

Daddy, you mean the world to me. You're an *ANGEL,* and I love you with all of my heart!

LOVE, HANA

MORE THAN A HERO

MUHAMMAD

His tongue has a silver lining;
his words are laced in gold.
His presence has been a gift from the heavens,
and his face is a sight to behold.
His accomplishments surpassed description,
as his faith broke through all dimensions,
his actions only glazed his intentions
and failed in comparison to his love.
His virtue never weakened when rested;
his honor never wavered when tested.
In his eyes lies a glimpse of God's heaven.
Through his laugh shines the glory of our nation.
His voice will not soon be forgotten,
nor his smile with its story of love.

A L I

You will never truly know
the depth of my father's soul,
how deep his dignity flows.
To love and give is all he knows.
His patience is a virtue of its own.
Your words are not gracious enough
to describe his taste.
Your colors just aren't lovely enough
to depict his face.
Honor is not sturdy enough
to uphold his name.
His soul has surpassed our humanly state.
A billion stars could never fulfill the space
his heart has sustained.
A million victories could never replace one moment
his soul has embraced.
No picture has ever sufficiently recaptured
the peace in his angelic eyes.
And no book will ever fully define
The beauty that Ali has devised.

HE IS MY FATHER, BUT YET A DREAM

What can I say that hasn't already been said?
What will I write that hasn't already been read?
And what can I show that hasn't already been seen?
These questions will be asked indeed; their answers firm and free . . .

I'll say:
He is my father, but yet a dream, for
if he were a lake, I'd be the stream.
If he were a root, I'd be his tree.
And if he were a fruit, I'd be the sweet.
I've only begun to enlighten thee . . .

For if he were a branch, I'd be his leaves.
If he were a plant, I'd be his seed.
If he were the wind, I'd be the breeze.
And if he were a sight, I'd be what's seen.

This is merely a glance of all I mean, for
if he were the sun, I'd be his rays.
If he were the dawn, I'd be the day.
If he were a trail, I'd be the way.
And if he were a tide, I'd be the wave.

He is my father, but yet a dream, for if he were an action,
I'd be the means.

Here you have a book to read, to glance at his inner mystery.
I'm part of what time will need to keep my father's spirit free.
I am here to share the story of a man whose heart has outshined glory.

As the world knows, my father grew up in a time when love was over-shadowed by hate, and fear was more dominant than faith. When United States blacks couldn't eat in certain restaurants or drink from water fountains that weren't labeled COLORED. Knowledge of our history allowed my father to prevail during those times. As a championship boxer, by example he helped salvage the confidence and love of all people suffering from racial oppression. He knew that in life we would always be faced with tragedy, loss, hatred, setbacks, and, at times, immense brutality and pain. He knew that it was the response to these encounters that would shape who he and we were to become as a people. My dad always said, "It's not the action that makes a thing right or wrong, but the purpose behind the action." A great person will somehow manage to hold on to the higher power throughout these rough times.

He kept his eyes on the prize. He conquered his fears with faith, he challenged his opponents gracefully, and he loved tremendously. I think it is more than safe to say that my father is more than a three-time heavyweight champion of the world, he's more than the "Greatest," more than an inspiration, more than the athlete of the century. He's a prophet, a messenger of God, an angel. He is a walking reflection of love and light. He's my father and he is my hero.

We have come a long way. However far our journey in life takes

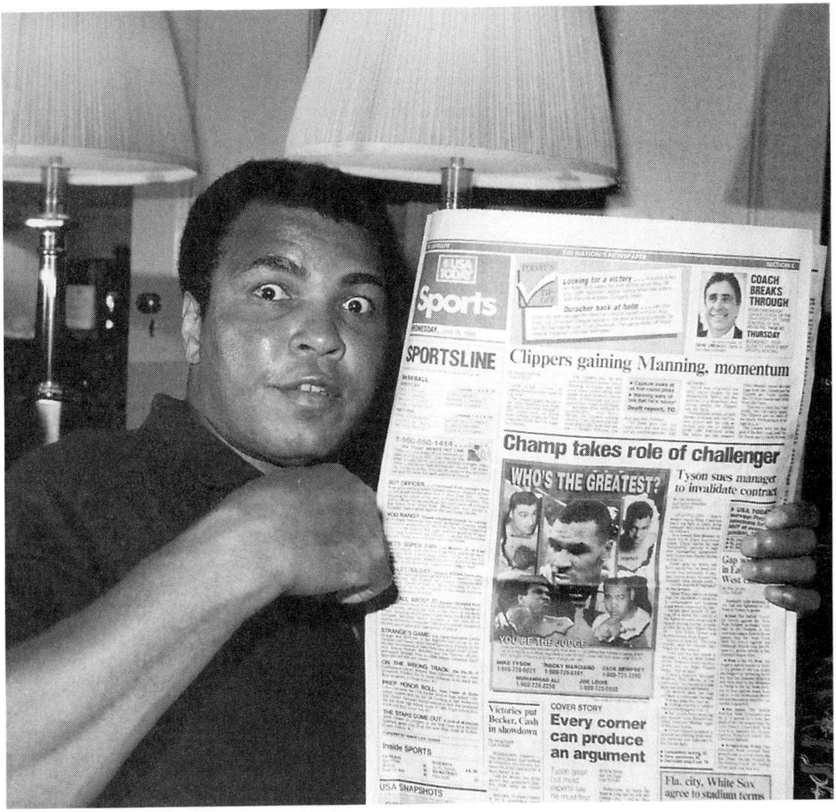

© Howard Bingham

us, however rocky the roads ahead may become or however rough the winds of heaven blow—we must never lose sight of faith and never let go of love. Grasp them both tightly, and hold on for dear life. We must never forget that we were all put here with a personal mission: To give love and to be loved, we must love our alikeness along with our differences. We must respect one another and cherish every day we have with the people we love. There has never been a storm turbulent enough to shake my father's unwavering faith in himself or his uninhibited love for all people everywhere. My advice to the world is to watch him, study him. If you follow his path, you will always be around the corner from heaven's gates.

© Howard Bingham

Dad in his office in Berrien Springs, Michigan.

IF YOU WANT TO LOSE YOUR
MONEY, THEN BET ON SONNY

MUHAMMAD ALI

If you want to lose your money,
then bet on Sonny.
He knows I'm great.
He went to school; he's no fool.

I predict that he will go in eight,
to prove that I'm great.
And if he wants to go to heaven,
I'll get him in seven.

He'll be in a worser fix if I cut it to six.
And if he keeps talking jive,
I'll cut it to five.
And if he makes me sore,
he'll go like Archie Moore, in four.

And if that don't do,
I'll cut it to two.

And if he run,

he'll go in one.

And if he don't want to fight,

he should keep his ugly self home that night.

AWARENESS

My father taught me not to idolize the material aspects of this world, but rather to appreciate the more essential qualities that life has to offer. He taught me that physical beauty and wealth were not among these aspects. He taught me to put my heart and soul into what was important and never to praise or rely on anything that could fade, be lost, or taken away. He taught me that the greatest prize of all is the awareness and acceptance of one's self—and that a person with a grand heart and the best of intentions possesses a true and everlasting beauty. He taught me that my faith, good nature, and goodwill could never be taken away from me, and that in the end these were the things that were surely mine—they are all we truly possess. In the end, this is what we have to show. He taught me to be in this world but not of it.

I've learned that when our charity, graciousness, and love are well spent, we are as great as our hearts. He taught me that love locked in the heart is wasted love; a dream not pursued is a dream forsaken. He not only taught me these things through verbal wisdom, but also showed me through his everyday actions that his ethics and beliefs were not just casual words and moral opinions. They were who he was, and are who he has become. He lived through his inner being and loved with his whole heart, mind, and soul. He backed up every word, every story, and every lesson with truth. He showed me that

wise words spoken hold little weight in comparison to those portrayed through action.

He lived in dedication to his beliefs, and through the roughest of times, they never faded, wavered, or perished. He showed me that faith is easier to hold on to when the waves of life are flowing smoothly. The trick is to hold on to that faith on the eve of our darkest nights. He taught me that wisdom is only as wise as knowledge and there's always more to learn. Throughout my life, there has never been one moment that the presence of my father's angelic soul has gone uncherished. He is a gift from God. When I look into his eyes, I know what God meant.

My wife and I have mastered the understanding of our inner life, which makes our relationship so beautiful. It's a blessing from Allah, and I think that this is what all people are looking for.

—Muhammad Ali

THE ART
OF PERSONALITY

Muhammad Ali

It is not necessary for every man to be a musician, a prizefighter, a lawyer, but it is necessary for every man to acquire the art of personality in order to use it in his endeavors. The salesman's business depends solely on his personality. If he is rude or unsympathetic, the buyer will run away, hoping to never see him again. But very often, the salesman with the proper personality can make a person buy when he doesn't intend to.

There are four categories of personality: there's the walnut personality; the prune personality; the pomegranate personality, which is hard fruit, hard outside and inside; and the grape personality. The walnut personality is hard outside and soft inside. People who are hard to get to know, once you crack the nut, the inside is soft. They are fully developed. The prune personality is soft outside and hard inside. These people seem to attract you, but once you get to know them, you find out they are not what you thought they were inside. They are hard. The pomegranate personality is hard outside and hard inside. Always looking out for themselves, these people hardly ever have friends. The grape personalities are soft outside and soft inside; even the seeds are digestible. If you take a bowl of fruit and put it on the table, you find out that grapes are the most attractive fruit. If you

© Hana Ali

Dad in the backseat of his limousine, leaving Los Angeles International Airport.

hand a person a bowl of some pears, apples, oranges, peaches, pome-granates, and grapes, the average person that would have a fruit will grab the grapes. Grapes are the most attractive fruit. This is wisdom you're hearing. You never heard that before? Well, you never will hear it again.

Silence is golden when you can't think of a good answer.

— MUHAMMAD ALI

THE GIFT

My fondest memory of my childhood is perhaps the most simple of all. I can remember waking up very early in the morning, running over to Laila's room to get her up. Together we would run down the stairs into the kitchen, to make an "interesting" cup of coffee for Dad. We put any and every thing we could reach on the countertop into a cup. My father would always drink it all up, then kiss us and tell us how good it was.

After that Laila would lie by the fireplace and draw as I sat on Daddy's lap pretending to write in cursive.

Dad would save our scribbles, explaining that one day as adults we could use them to look back and appreciate the child we once were. I think that it was really my father's way of holding time still, savoring the moment. It was also his gift to us and his way of making us feel important, loved, and understood.

The greatest gift a parent can ever give to a child, my father gave to us time and time again—himself.

THE GIFT

Dear God,

Does this world see what we can see?

Do they know what we know?

Just how precious my father is, how sweetly his kind heart gives.

How graciously his tender soul lives.

Can they hear what I can hear?

When he smiles, he reflects more light

than all the stars that grace the sky's ails.

And when he laughs, he spreads great joy,

with all the world's most timid coy.

Thank you, God, for the gift.

My pleasures would have been fully lived

by simply knowing him.

But you went and blessed me further,

by granting me the honor of calling an angel my father.

My sister Laila reaching down to give my father
a kiss after winning her first professional fight.

One day, my father was driving down the highway in Los Angeles when he was pulled over by the police. He was given a one-hundred-dollar speeding ticket. Dad wrote the officer a check on the spot. When the officer looked at it, he said, "Mr. Ali, there's been a mistake. The ticket is only for a hundred dollars. You made this out for two." My father looked up at the officer with wide eyes and said, "I still have to come back."

We have one life; it soon will be past; what we do for God is all that will last.

—MUHAMMAD ALI

BELIEVING

Not too long ago my father, Lonnie, and I went to meet with Jon Peters, who is the producer of an upcoming movie on my father's life, in which Will Smith will be portraying him. Shortly after our arrival we all gathered in the living room of Jon's beautiful Beverly Hills home, had a few laughs, snacked a bit, then watched the previews of his most recent movie, *Wild Wild West*. Lonnie, later, popped some old footage of my father into the VCR. In complete silence we watched a three-minute interview my father did during the mid-sixties.

He was riding in the backseat of a New York taxicab when a young female reporter pulled up beside him and boldly asked, "What was it you would have done if you weren't a boxer?" As always, my father held his head up high before confidently replying, "Well, I would have been the world's greatest at whatever I did. If I were a garbageman, I'd be the world's greatest garbageman! I'd pick up more garbage and faster than anyone has ever seen. To tell you the truth, I would have been the world's greatest at whatever I'd done!"

BELIEVE

If there were a nightingale
who could bring its songs to life
and spread them among the universe
to free all hearts of strife,
my father would be sung.
And if ever there were an angel
who left a trail of prints
for all the world to follow them,
through rain and storm and wind,
my father would be him.

STILL THE GREATEST

MUHAMMAD ALI

Since I won't let critics seal my fate,
they keep hollering I'm full of hate.
But they don't really hurt me none
'cause I'm doing good and having fun.

And fun to me is something bigger
than what those critics fail to figure.
Fun to me is lots of things
and along with it some good I bring.

Yet while I'm busy helping my people,
these critics keep writing I'm deceitful.
But I can take it on my chin,
And that's the honest truth, my friend.

Now from Muhammad you just heard
the latest and the truest word.
So when they ask you, What's the latest?
just say, Ask Ali, he's still the Greatest.

To be able to give away riches is mandatory if you wish to possess them. This is the only way that you will be truly rich.

—MUHAMMAD ALI

THE LESSON

One day I asked my father why he kept the people that he knew had stolen from him in his life for so long. He didn't answer me right away; he was staring down at the floor with a puzzled look on his face. Finally, after heaving a long sigh, he said, "Hana, we are all only human. We all have committed sins—some big, some small. In the end, we all ask God for forgiveness; then we turn our back on our fellow men when they are in need of forgiveness. If God forgives, we too should forgive. Everyone deserves a second chance. Everyone is trying to live the best they can with the hand that they've been dealt. It's not always easy. Life is not equally kind to us all. Remember to treat everyone with respect and equality, and God will always bless you."

A SHORT SPEECH

MUHAMMAD ALI

I have found in life that most people get pleasure out of knowing that they have something that other people don't. When we follow the rule of God and religion, it teaches that we should want for our brother what we want for ourselves. I'm not happy driving a Rolls-Royce and living up on a hill when I know that my brothers and sisters are hungry in a soup line.

I'm the world champion, but I don't feel I'm any different from a fan. I'll still walk in the ghettos, answer questions, and kiss babies. I'll never forget my people.

I don't have to be what anyone else wants me to be. I am free to be who I want to be.

—MUHAMMAD ALI

BLACK PRIDE

Muhammad Ali

I woke up this morning feeling good and black.
I got out my black bed;
I put on my black robe,
played all my best black records,
and drank some good black coffee.
Then I put on my black shoes,
walked out my black door,
and, oh Lord, white snow!

A MESSAGE TO MY PEOPLE

MUHAMMAD ALI

This is a speech that was delivered on the black college circuit during my father's exile from boxing.

I believe it is very important to teach our people more about our history. We can never be free until we know about ourselves. This is the reason The Book says you should know the truth and the truth alone shall make you free. It doesn't say segregation or education; it says the truth shall make you free. There is a lot of great truth in black history. We look at television and we see the white-tornado floor wax and everything is white. Although a tornado is black, they made it white. And we see that Miss America is white, Miss Universe is white, and Miss World.

We go to church, look at pictures of Jesus Christ, and we see a white man. We look at the Last Supper and we see all white people. There are no Chinese at the Last Supper, no Indians, and no Sudanese, all white people. We look at Tarzan in the jungle of hot-ass Africa, and he's white. We look at the angels in heaven, all white angels, no black angels, no Mexican angels. I imagine they died and went to heaven too. When they took pictures, I heard that all the black angels were in the kitchen preparing milk and honey!

Our people see all this "white" and hear nothing good about "black." The black cat gives bad luck; blackguard is the bad lot; the ugly duckling is a black duck; a threat of blackmail; blackballed from a fraternity. Black is associated with all things bad, which makes our people feel like nothing. Black history is badly needed for us to realize that there is no Tarzan in Africa, and if there were a Tarzan, he would be black, not white.

Before God created the heaven and earth, The Book says everything was in darkness; then God said let there be light! Before God was "creating," there was black on the scene.

Once our people learn that a black man, Benjamin Banneker, helped in designing Washington, D.C.; that Charles Drew, a black man, developed methods for preserving and transporting blood and plasma; that a black man invented traffic lights, and so many other great things, they will be proud. It is important that in our libraries we have books on black history so we can read more about ourselves. The Chinese people read about themselves; the Indians read about themselves; white people read about themselves; and Puerto Ricans know all about their history. We need to know our history and accomplishments. However, we know about everybody else's history but not our own.

BLACK HAS A RIGHTFUL PLACE

Muhammad Ali

Everything they should find—
Rich dirt is black dirt,
Strong coffee is black coffee,
Blacker the berries the sweeter the juice.
Ain't nothing wrong—
Black is the original, black is first,
Black has a rightful place.

REMEMBERING

This past weekend, at my father's fifty-seventh birthday, Gene Kelroy, one of his oldest friends, related a special memory of my father. It went something like this: A few weeks before the 1974 fight in Zaire, where Dad would fight to win back the title, he received a phone call concerning a little boy who was in the hospital with leukemia. Right away, Dad jumped on the next flight out, went to the boy's hospital, and walked straight up to his room and gave him a kiss and hug. Then he looked him in the eye and said, "I am going to Africa and win back my title. I'm going to win my battle. And you're going to win yours."

Shortly after that, Dad flew back to the training camp and eventually went to Africa, where he won back the heavyweight championship. Not long after he returned, Dad got a second phone call from the boy's parents. They congratulated him on his victory and then explained that it didn't look as if the boy was going to make it. Once again, Dad was on the next flight out. When he arrived, he walked right to the boy's bedside. "I told you that we were going to win our battles together. I won mine; now you are going to win yours."

The boy looked up at him and said, "No, I'm going to heaven to meet God, and I'm going to tell him that I knew you, and that you were my friend."

My way of joking is to tell the truth.
That's the funniest joke in the world.

—MUHAMMAD ALI

A few years ago I was at a dinner party with my father and a few of my sisters. Toward the end of the evening a man from the audience walked up to the microphone and shared a memory of my father with us all. Before the man finished his final words, I reached over to kiss my father's cheek. He had tears in his eyes.

The man opened with a short speech reflecting back on the good old days. Apparently he had accompanied my father on one of the many fight promotional tours. One day they stopped at a senior citizens' home to visit someone who was a longtime fan. Before my dad made it out of the lobby, a ninety-nine-year-old man whispered, "I know who you are."

"Who am I?" asked my father.

"You're the greatest boxer that ever lived."

"What's my name?"

"Your name is Joe Louis. I've seen all your fights, and I'm honored to meet you."

One of the people with my father started to say, "You crazy old . . ." Before he could finish his sentence, my dad pulled him aside and said, "Man, this guy is ninety-nine years old. His eyesight is probably failing him; his hearing is almost gone. I'm sure he lived a hard life working hard just to put food on the table. Now he's old and tired and probably doesn't have much longer to live. If Joe Louis is who he thinks he sees and that's who he wants me to be, then let's leave him his pride. Tonight I'm just going to be Joe Louis."

Jones likes to mix

so I'll let it go in six.

If he talks jive,

I'll cut it to five.

And if he talks some more,

I'll cut it to four.

And if he talks about me,

I'll cut it to three.

And if that don't do,

I'll cut it to two.

And if you want some fun,

I'll cut it to one.

And if he don't want to fight,

he can stay home that night.

—MUHAMMAD ALI

THE GLORY DAYS

I remember Laila, Dad, and I driving down Wilshire Boulevard in Los Angeles when I was a little girl. We were in Dad's brown Rolls-Royce. The top was down, as usual, and I can still feel the wind blowing my hair against my face. My dad loved that car, and still has it in the garage of his home in Berrien Springs, Michigan. Every summer, Dad would fly in the rest of our brothers and sisters—who weren't living with us, since they were all from other marriages. There were eight of us in total; now that Asaad has come along, there are nine. At eight years old, Asaad is the youngest. Anyway, we'd often all pile into the car and go driving all around Los Angeles—with the top down. People on the road would see Dad and shout out: "Hi, Champ!" "You're the Greatest!" or "Oh, my God, it's Muhammad Ali!" Those were the Glory Days.

I think it's wonderful how my father always made sure that all his children knew and loved one another. On the occasions when we would fight or when we simply weren't getting along, he would cry and tell us that we were supposed to love and protect each other, not fight or be jealous of what the other person has.

One time, when it was just Dad and I on our way back from Carnations (Dad's favorite restaurant back then), he noticed a homeless man being thrown out of another restaurant. He made a U-turn and pulled up right in front of the man. Dad got out of the car, and before he could open his mouth, the man shouted out, "Oh, my God, I must have died and gone to heaven, either that or my eyes are playing tricks on me." My father replied, "You're not in heaven yet, and your eyes are working fine. It's me."

The man shook my father's hand as he explained that he was homeless and only trying to get something to eat, but the manager wouldn't give him a seat. My father got me out of the car, walked the man right back into the restaurant, where he looked into the eyes of the manager on duty and said, "This man is hungry, he has no place to call home, and no food to eat. He is a human being. Since he's worthy enough to occupy space on God's earth, he certainly is worthy enough to eat in this restaurant."

The three of us sat at a booth with the man while he ate his food. When he was through, Dad drove him to a hotel and paid the bill in advance for one month. He then told him to get cleaned up and he would help him find a good job.

A L I

You will never truly know the depth of my father's soul,

how deep his dignity flows. To love and give is all he knows,

and his patience is a virtue of its own.

Your words are not gracious enough to describe his taste.

Your colors just aren't lovely enough to depict his face.

Honor is not sturdy enough to uphold his name.

His soul has surpassed our humanly state.

A billion stars could never fulfill the space his heart has sustained.

A million victories could never replace one moment

his soul has embraced.

No picture has ever sufficiently captured the peace

in his angelic eyes.

And no book will ever fully define the beauty that Ali has devised.

Dad and me in Laila's dressing room the night of her first fight.

Love is a net that catches hearts like a fish.

— MUHAMMAD ALI

THE HEART OF MAN

Muhammad Ali

The personality of a person is formed around the heart, and the heart is a piece of flesh hidden in the breast. The heart is the sum of a person around which his personality is born. Consciously or unconsciously man loves the word "heart." And if we were to ask a poet to write his poems and not use the word "heart," he would not satisfy himself or others. Yet the poets who have appealed the most to humanity have used the word "heart" the most in their poems. For what is a man? A man is his heart; a dead heart means a dead man; a living heart means a living man.

People look for wonders, for miracles—look for surprises of all kinds. Yet the greatest surprise is to be found in one's heart. The greatness or the smallness of a man does not depend on his outer things. Regardless of how wealthy a man may be, or how great, if his heart is not great, then he cannot be great. But if his heart is great, then he remains great under all circumstances. It is the heart that makes one great or small.

Hearts can be of all different kinds. There is the golden heart, the silver heart, some with copper, and some with iron. How do these hearts differ in quality? The golden heart shows its color, its beauty, and at the same time, it is soft, precious, and valuable; the silver heart shows inferior qualities compared to the golden heart. Yet, coins are made out of silver, and silver is more useful than gold.

Dad in the backseat of his limousine.

Of the copper heart, pennies too are useful. They are more useful than silver or gold coins. Copper is strong and hard and needs many hammers to beat and make something out of it. Then there's the heart of iron, which must be put into a hot fire before anything can be done with it. And the iron becomes hot and soft in the glowing fire, and we can make something out of it. But the blacksmith must always be ready once the iron begins to melt in the glowing flame. He must start working at once. If he lets it go, it will turn cold immediately. Then there is the heart of rock that must be broken before anything can be done with it. A cold heart, neither rain nor water has much effect on the heart of rock. But when the heart is of wax, like mine or that of nice people who want to help others, it melts as soon as sunlight or anything nice falls upon it. And when heated, one can mold it any way one wishes.

Then there is the heart of paper, which flies like a kite in the wind to the north, to the south, to the east, and to the west. One can control the heart of paper as long as the string is strong enough to hold it. But when there is no wind, it drops down. There are many, many more kinds of hearts; each different in quality. Once we begin to distinguish the qualities of the actions of the heart, we begin to see living miracles in every moment of our lives. Is there anything that can be compared to the heart? It lives and it dies. Yet it is revived and it lives again. Then it dies again.

The heart can be torn, and it can be mended repeatedly. It can be broken, and it can be made whole again. It can rise and it can fall; and it can fall and it can rise; and after rising, it can fall again instantly. There is one heart that can creep. There is another heart that can walk. There is another heart that can run. And there's another heart that can fly. Yet, we cannot limit its action.

If we depict the heart as a hot glowing ball of fire, we can see the different aspects of love in the form of the heart: sympathy in the form of flame; passion in the form of smoke that blinds one's eyes. If we were to look at what gives us the strength to stand strong in the battlefield, to endure all that may come, that which gives us the power to have patience, what is it? It is the heart. If the heart fails, one fails. If the heart rises, one rises. When the heart is directed at one object, one purpose, one romance, then it is strengthened. But when the heart goes from one object to another, one religion to another, one movement, one organization, one love—then the fire elements die. The heart dies.

When a man says, "I love everybody," you can be sure that he don't love nobody! When he says, "I love my mother, I love my brother, I love my sister, I love my beloved," then he is taking the first step on the road of love. Many of us today have asked about love and we don't know the true meaning of love. The meaning of love is the feeling that one is alive. That feeling itself is love. What is love? Love is God, and God is love.

BYE-BYE, VEGGIES

When I was a little girl, my sister Laila and I were always served a full-course meal. I, like most little people, despised vegetables. However, Laila loved vegetables the way I enjoy butter pecan ice cream. On occasion my father would come into the room where we ate, which was around the corner and down the hall from his office, and he'd hug and kiss us—then he would eat my vegetables for me. And when he was full or didn't feel like eating them, or after spending an hour or so trying to convince me that they were good, or when bribing me with thirty-one flavors of ice cream just didn't seem to work, he would sneak me around to the corner bathroom and let me flush them down the toilet.

My father the hero and every little boy's and girl's dream: a parent who helped them dispose of their vegetables.

My sister Laila and me on the night of her first professional fight.

IS A DOLLAR TOO MUCH?

Not too long ago, I was sitting in the kitchen with my dad at his house in Berrien Springs, Michigan. He was eating a peanut-butter-and-jelly sandwich that I had just made for him. Shortly after finishing it, he asked me to get him a glass of milk. He looked at me with questioning eyes and said, "Hana, this is a pretty good meal, isn't it? I was just thinking; I'd like to open a restaurant in every major town, where the homeless and people earning low incomes could go eat for free or a very low price—and our specialty would be peanut-butter-and-jelly sandwiches with a tall glass of milk. Would you order it?"

"Yes, I would. I love peanut-butter-and-jelly sandwiches."

He smiled at me. "That's it! An all-you-can-eat menu with nothing priced over a dollar. A house specialty of two peanut-butter-and-jelly sandwiches and a tall ice-cold glass of milk." Then he gave me a puzzled look and asked, "You think a dollar is too much?"

You know, I think it's amazing how, in the midst of all that generosity, he still felt that there was more that he could give. Is a dollar too much?

FAITH

Muhammad Ali

I am riding on my horse of hope,
holding in my hand the rein of courage.
Dressed in the armor of patience,
with the helmet of endurance on my head,
I started out on my journey to the land of love.

PURPOSE

As a little boy, my father knew that he was here for a special purpose. When he was nine years old, he would get up one hour earlier than he had to. He would go outside and sit on the front porch of his house. He would look up at the sky and wait for God to tell him his mission in life. He went on this way for a few years.

I recently asked him if this was true. When he replied in the affirmative, I inquired as to what made him stop. He said, "I never heard anything."

© Howard Bingham

Back row, left to right: *Daddy, Rashidah, Jamillah, May May, and Mia.*
Front row, left to right: *Khaliah, Muhammad Jr., Laila, and me.*

THE PURPOSE OF LIFE

MUHAMMAD ALI

This speech is the first of many given by my father during the three and one-half years after his title was taken and his right to fight revoked in 1967, because of his refusal to take the step that would enroll him in the United States Army (which in my eyes is where his heroism lies—in his bravery to do what he believes in, no matter what). Following this, he was offered professorships at Oxford University and at Harvard University and other leading colleges, where he would give his remarkable poetry and influential speeches life.

Every living being was born to accomplish a certain purpose. It is the knowledge of the purpose that enables every soul to fulfill it. Ten persons with the knowledge of the purpose of their lives are more powerful than one thousand working from morning until evening. Besides what we call right or wrong, good or bad, are differences according to the purpose of life. The more we study a situation, we find out that it is not action that makes a thing right or wrong but the purpose of the action.

Everything that God created was put here for a purpose. The rain has a purpose; trees have a purpose; the moon, pigs, sheep, fish of the sea, insects, everything has a purpose; and most surely this is true—which it is true—man has a purpose too. Brothers and sisters, you must find out what your life purpose is. Once you find this purpose, a switch is turned and light is on. What is your purpose? What is my purpose? The moment we begin to ask ourselves this question, we have begun to take the first step on the path to wisdom. Because the very secret of life is to accomplish something. An absence of this desire makes life useless. Hope is the ingredient of life; hope comes from the determination to achieve something; therefore, the determination in itself can be a very great power. The goal, which the purpose is seeking to reach, can be small in comparison to the power he gains in the process of his determination, because without the power to be determined, the goal can never be reached.

Regardless of how small or how large the purpose, you were all born to accomplish a certain purpose. And, it is the knowing of that purpose that enables every soul to fulfill it. A wise man is he who knows his life purpose, so we should know this purpose in childhood. Parents overlook this, considering other things more important; but very few of them realize that it is in one's childhood that one must discover one's life purpose, because life is awful short. Why were you born? My purpose was to be the world's heavyweight champion who was free to do as he believed. That was my purpose, but I had to pay a price. I had to give up three and one-half years of my life to stay on track and then was sentenced to five years in jail. The greater the sacrifice, the greater the gain. Once you find that purpose, obstacles on the left, obstacles on the right, from the front or behind, should not hinder. Your purpose may not be as big as mine or another man's purpose. God will not place a burden on a man's shoulders knowing that he cannot carry it. Whatever your purpose, no matter how small, commit to the determination of that purpose.

THUNDER

MUHAMMAD ALI

I done wrestled with an alligator,
I done tussled with a whale.
Handcuffed lightning,
and threw thunder in jail.
I can run through a hurricane
and not get wet.
Only last week,
I murdered a rock,
I injured a stone,
hospitalized a brick.
I'm so mean I make medicine sick.

A BEDTIME STORY

When I was just a little girl, no more than eight or nine years old, I can remember crying myself to sleep the nights my parents weren't home. Although I eventually got used to their absence, I never really understood that their leaving had nothing to do with their love for us. Later I came to realize that sometimes parents have to spend a little time away. It didn't matter where they went or how far they went, they still loved us and carried us with them in their hearts.

One of my favorite childhood memories is of a bedtime story my dad would tell me. On the nights when I had trouble sleeping, which was quite often, I would run down the hall to my father's bedroom and he would tell me all kinds of wonderful stories until I fell asleep. My favorite of those stories was "A Slave Named Omar."

Once upon a time, there was a slave named Omar. He was no ordinary slave. Omar was something special. One day the king called a town meeting that everyone in the town was expected to attend, including the slaves. In the middle of the king's speech, he spotted Omar in the crowd and knew that there was something special about him. He pointed him out and asked him to come up to the platform, instantly appointing him his personal helper. Omar was given a brand-new beautiful wardrobe, jewelry, and a big luxurious bedroom right next to the king's chambers. Omar was happy.

After a few weeks passed, one of the other king's men grew jeal-

© Tim Shanahan

Dad and me.

ous of Omar because of how close he and the king were becoming. One day this man woke up early and decided to spy on Omar, hoping to find something negative on him that he could report back to the king. On his way down the hall he noticed that Omar was already up, carrying a big red sack over his shoulders and heading straight for the king's treasure room. He followed Omar and waited outside the doors in amazement until Omar came out. After he saw that Omar came out with the same big sack he went in with, the man ran to the king and told him that Omar was stealing his treasures. The king asked him how he knew this.

"I saw him with my own eyes. You see, Your Highness, I've been watching him for some time now, and every morning he gets up an hour earlier than everyone else, goes into your treasure room with a big sack over his back, and then he comes out with it and heads back to his room."

The king replied, "I shall follow him myself."

The very next morning the king waited outside Omar's room, and sure enough, he came out with a big red sack and walked right into the treasure room. The king followed and watched Omar as he put down the bag and opened it up. Omar took off his princely robes and then pulled out his old slave robe from the bag, put it on, stood in front of the mirror, and said to himself, "Omar, just yesterday you were a slave sleeping in the streets with very little food to eat. Today you are living in the king's castle, wearing beautiful clothes, with all the food you can ever need. Never forget where you came from—just as easily as it was given, it can be taken away. Never forget who you are or how blessed you have been." Omar then took off his slave robe, placed it back in the bag, and put on his princely robes. As he headed for the door, he saw the king, who was in tears.

The king put his hands on Omar's shoulders. "Omar, I followed you here because I thought you were stealing from me. I've never been more ashamed in my life. I should have known better. I knew there was something special about you the very first time I spotted you in the crowd. I was right. Omar, you've taught me something very important today that I will always remember. Although I may be the king, you have a king's heart."

Dad still tells the story of Omar. Before he can ever finish it, though, he is in tears.

THE LEGEND OF CASSIUS CLAY

MUHAMMAD ALI

This is the legend of Cassius Clay,
the most beautiful fighter in the world today.
He talks a great deal and brags indeedly
of a muscular punch
that's incredibly speedy.
This fistic world was dull and weary;
with a champ like Liston,
things had to be dreary.
Then someone with color,
someone with dash,
brought the fight fans
running with cash.
This brash young boxer is something to see,
and the heavyweight championship is his destiny.

It isn't the mountains ahead to climb that wear you out; it's the pebble in your shoe.

—Muhammad Ali

H E A L I N G

MUHAMMAD ALI

If you love God, you can't separate out only some of his children to love. To be against people because they're Muslim is wrong. To be against people because they're Jewish or Christian is wrong. To be against people because they're black or white or yellow or brown is wrong. Anyone who believes in one God should also believe that all people are part of one family. People are people. God created us all. And all people have to work to get along.

My mother was a Baptist. She believed that Jesus was the son of God. I don't believe that. But even though my mother had a religion different from mine, I believe that on Judgment Day my mother will be in heaven. If you're a good Muslim, if you're a good Christian, Jew, . . . you'll receive God's blessing.

When I was young, I followed a teaching that disrespected other people and said that white people were "devils." I was wrong. Color doesn't make a man a devil. It's the heart and mind and soul that count. *When God makes someone, the most important part is the heart and soul. What's on the outside is only decoration.* Hating people because of their color is wrong. And it doesn't matter which color does the hating. It's just plain wrong. *Muslims, Christians, Jews, people of all religions, have different ways of worshipping God; but we're all trying to get to the same place.*

If I hated, I couldn't think. If I hated, I couldn't eat. If I hated, I couldn't work. I'd be frustrated. I don't hate. *I just wish people would love everybody else the way that they love me. It would be a better world.*

© Howard Bingham

Dad and me at home in Los Angeles.

I AM THE GREATEST

MUHAMMAD ALI

Clay comes out to meet Liston,
and Liston starts to retreat.
If Liston starts to retreat any further,
he'll end up in a ringside seat.
Clay swings with a left.
Clay swings with a right.
Look at young Cassius
carry the fight.
Liston keeps backing,
but there's not enough room.
It's a matter of time —
There, Clay lowers the boom.
Now Clay swings with a right.
What a beautiful swing.
And the punch raises the bear
clear out of the ring.

Liston is still rising,
and the ref wears a frown.
For he can't start counting

till Sonny comes down.
Now Liston disappears from view.
The crowd is getting frantic,
but our radar stations have picked him up.
He's somewhere over the Atlantic.
Who would have thought
when they came to the fight
that they'd witness the launching
of a human satellite.
Yes, the crowd did not dream
when they laid down their money
that they would see
a total eclipse of the Sonny.
I am the Greatest!

MEMORIES

MARYUM ALI

When I was a little girl, my father and I were walking through downtown Chicago. A sea of excited fans surged around him in hope of getting his autograph. As usual, Daddy tried to accommodate them all. Later that day, he noticed he was missing five thousand dollars from his coat pocket. Someone had picked his pocket during the crush that day. When my father's manager scolded him about being more responsible with his money, Daddy replied, "I don't care about that money. The person who stole it probably needed it for their rent or to feed their children. That money will help someone, and that makes me feel good."

MEMORIES

MARYUM ALI

When I was twenty-nine years old, with a marriage on the verge of divorce, I went to my father for advice. I said, "Daddy, it doesn't look good. My husband is acting up pretty bad."

My dad told me, "Well, if you think you've done everything you can do and the marriage still isn't working out, make sure you keep your eyes open."

"Keep my eyes open?" I said, confused.

With a sly look on his face, Daddy answered, "When you go to prayer service on Friday, keep your eyes open and you may find your next husband."

Here I am thinking my father would express major disappointment, but instead he said something that sent me laughing out of my seat.

"I should have expected a statement like that from someone who's been married four times," I said as we both laughed.

Wisdom is knowing when you can't be wise.

—MUHAMMAD ALI

Dad and me in Chicago.

THE RECIPE FOR LIFE

MUHAMMAD ALI

Take a few cups of love,
one teaspoon of patience,
one tablespoon of generosity,
one pint of laughter,
one quart of intelligence,
one sprinkle of concern,
and then mix willingness, and add lots of faith.
Mix it all up.
Spread it over the span of a lifetime,
and serve it to each and every deserving person you meet.

SHOW-AND-TELL

On occasion, when I was growing up, before my parents got divorced, Dad would put Laila and me on the school bus in the morning—on the days that we weren't driven to school, that is. Once a week, on Friday, we had show-and-tell at school. One Friday morning, I woke up and put on my favorite little white dress. It had ruffles all around the edges with a little white bow in the front. I grabbed all my fancy dolls out of the cabinet and put on some of my jewelry given to me by my mother. I wasn't supposed to take any of it to school or wear it in the swimming pool or wear it while outside playing. Being the mischievous child that I was, I was set on taking the jewelry to school, anyway.

When my father saw me sashaying down the driveway, he looked at me, smiled, and then he gave me a little lecture. He said, "Hana, you look very pretty, just like your mother, but not everyone is as fortunate as you and your sister are. You shouldn't wear your prettiest clothing to school or take your most expensive toys to show-and-tell. It might make the kids whose parents can't afford to buy them gifts like these feel bad. If everyone isn't happy, there just wouldn't be much joy in show-and-tell, now would there? When you can, try not to flaunt what you have in front of anyone, especially those who you know are less fortunate than you; then God will always bless you."

THE RISE

Hana Ali

I will not bow my head in shame,
I will not blend within my pain.
I'm going to rise above my fears
and free the clouds that sealed my tears.
I'm going to rise for all lost years
and steer a storm that never clears.
I'm going to lock my fears behind,
and from this day forth, I'm going to climb.
I'm going as far as life will take me.
I will not let this world shake me.
Only God can make or break me.
I'm going to reach that mountain high
that our leaders viewed through dreamy eyes,
and prophets spoke of from heavenly skies.
I'm going to bank on faith and glide.
Through rain or storm, I'm going to climb.
But before my venture begins to ride,
I'm going to start with reaching inside.
And I'm going to lend my heart a hand,
because this is where all journeys begin.
And love is where all paths end.

COMEBACK NIGHT

MUHAMMAD ALI

You may talk about Sweden, you may talk about Rome,
but Rockville Center's Floyd Patterson's home.
A lot of people said that Floyd couldn't fight,
but you should have seen him on the comeback night.

THE GIFT OF A MEMORY

Old friends of my mother and father's recently called me to catch up on old times—Tim and Helga Shannahan. We hadn't spoken in nine years, so we had a lot of catching up to do. They were more than surprised to find out that my best friend and roommate is boxer Ken Norton's daughter. A lot of people seem to find the situation hilarious, Muhammad Ali's and Ken Norton's daughters living together. I guess it is a little ironic.

Tim shared one of his memories of my father and me: One day when I was about three and a half years old, I was crying because my dad had to leave town to train for an upcoming fight. To stop me from crying he picked me up, sat me on his lap, and said "I'm your daddy, but sometimes, I'm the daddy to the rest of the world too. But when I leave, I take you with me in my heart." My father then turned to Tim, telling him that when he looked at me, it was like looking at himself.

Tim shared another incident: I was about five, and my father was preparing to leave for yet another fight. Once again, I was upset. I locked myself in my room, refusing to say good-bye to my dad. Dad asked Tim if he would go up and try to convince me to come down. When Tim walked into my room, he told me that my father loved me and wouldn't leave until I kissed him good-bye. "He's not my daddy; he's Muhammad Ali," I shouted. Tim returned downstairs and relayed my statement back to my father, who was moved to tears. When I heard him crying, I ran straight down the stairs and right into my father's arms to kiss him good-bye.

FREE TO BE ME

MUHAMMAD ALI

Why does everybody attack me for being righteous? What it boils down to is a matter of fear. Do I fear the almighty government more, or do I fear God? I fear God more.

If I had to give up my fighting or my religion, I already know what I would do. I would give up boxing and never look back! No Vietcong ever called me a nigger. I am not going to war.

Every day, they die in Vietnam for nothing. I might as well stay right here for something! If going to war—and possibly dying— would help twenty-two million Negroes gain freedom, justice, and equality, I would not have to be drafted. I would join tomorrow.

I want peace, and I do not find peace in a segregated world. I love to be black, and I love to be with my people.

I don't have to be what anyone else wants me to be. I am free to be who I want to be . . .

Dad and me at Deer Lake Training Camp.

THE CHALLENGE

Toward the end of my parents' marriage, when I was about nine years old, my need to be with my father increased. I would wake up earlier than everyone else, run outside, and hide in the backseat of the car so that I could spend the day with him. For a long while, I got away with it. Dad wouldn't discover me back there until I giggled or he reclined his seat back, causing me to shout out, "Ouch!"

I loved being with my father. Pretty soon it got out of hand, and if I reached my father before the governess or my mother could get to me, they knew that I would cry and my dad wouldn't be able to tell me no. It would be another day I was going to school late, if at all. After a while, when this became a problem, the governess had a little latch put at the top of my bedroom door. It didn't stop me. I would climb up the bookshelf that was beside my door and unlock it. After that plan failed, she tried tying a stocking from my outer doorknob to the third-floor staircase. That too didn't seem to work; I would just pull the door back with all of my might and slip right out—making it to my father. Later, she used a rope instead. Lucky for me, her room was joined to mine. When I couldn't slip through that one, I crawled very quietly out of my room, passing by her to exit on the other side. Again, I made it to my father.

After a while Dad explained to me that I had to go to school and that he would be home before I got back. We could then spend the remainder of the day together.

My mom, Veronica, and Dad dancing at their wedding in 1977.

FLYING ALONE

A few months ago I went to Michigan to visit my father. Everybody who knows me well knows how afraid I am to fly alone. It had been prearranged for me to take a flight out of Los Angeles with my dad, but something happened and I would have to take the flight alone. I was extremely nervous. I'm twenty-three years young and was then twenty-two and had never flown alone. My stepmother, Lonnie, had called me up to break the news. After saying everything she could to make me feel okay with it, she put my father on the phone.

When Dad picked up the line, he instantly said, "Hana, you have nothing to be afraid of. You're my daughter, so God takes extra care of you." I told him that didn't do it for me and I would just feel more comfortable if someone were flying with me. He then paused before saying, "Well, just think about this. If your plane goes down and you bring a friend, they're going to die too." As blunt as that statement was, I saw the logic in it—and from then on, I've been flying alone.

I MADE MY PLAY

MUHAMMAD ALI

I made my play,
and I'm going all the way.
So I'm happy,
and I wake up happy.
And if I go to jail tomorrow,
I'll go to jail happy.
Because eighty percent of the prisoners in there are brothers,
and they're waiting to be tough too.
I'd convert the whole jail.

Back row, left to right: *Rashidah, Jamillah, May May, and Mia.*
Front row, left to right: *Muhammad Jr., me, Dad, Khaliah, and
Laila. We are on the front lawn of our house in Los Angeles.*

FOLLOW THE LEADER

One bright summer day, I woke up a little earlier than normal—five o'clock in the morning. I got dressed and walked downstairs. The house was a little quiet. I noticed a cup of coffee sitting on my father's desk next to a stack of opened fan mail. I decided to go look for him. By the time I made it halfway through the kitchen, I spotted him in the driveway. He was bending over as if he were looking at something very closely. I decided to stand there and watch him for a moment. And I did. About every sixty seconds or so he would move a few inches, still bending over while looking straight down. I walked out of the kitchen door and headed for the very spot where he was standing.

Before I could open my mouth, he whispered, "Be careful, you might step on them." I asked, "Step on what?" He told me to walk carefully over to the other side of him. Then I saw them: a trail of ants. They were all lined up single-file, seemingly headed for the grass. I looked at my father in amazement and asked how long he had been out there and what he was doing. After a brief pause he stood up, stretched before looking at me with wide eyes, and said, "I'm watching. I've been out here for about an hour now, and it has taken that trail of ants that long to get from there to here." He pointed to a big tree about fifteen feet across the driveway. "They're all following the ant in front. Some of them have ventured off on their own and others have just stopped, but the majority of them are still going. They're all following the ant at the head of the line."

Then, as we walked back toward the kitchen door, my dad looked at me and said, "I'm like a little ant. Lots of other little ants know me; they follow me. So God gives me some extra power."

I once asked my father if he would rather be the smartest man in the world, with a little heart, or a man of common knowledge who had a heart of gold. He turned to me and said, "The man with all the knowledge, but with a little heart, he can only get so far. The man with all the love awaits the open doors of heaven."

My father told me something else that I will never forget. He said that one of the problems with the world today is that while we're busy making sure our children gain basic knowledge that will help them through this life, we neglect the more important lessons that they will need to make them better individuals—such as knowing how to be a true friend or caring about the less fortunate. We're so caught up in trying to make the grade that we forget to nourish our soul. As important as it is to acquire the knowledge that we need to help us live comfortably, we won't need to know how to spell or subtract in heaven—and it's not the size of our bank account that gets us there. It's the size of our heart.

He then told me to stay in school and work hard, but to never forget that I can only go as far as my heart has loved.

In the way he has carried the weight of all the adulation that he's embraced. In the way he's managed to reach the mountaintop and never look down upon anyone. In the way he loves with his whole heart, without discriminating or rejecting the weak or lost. In the way he'll sit and sign every last autograph, until his hands are tired, or our plane has taken off. Without us in it! And in the way he stares at poverty until he's blue in the face. In the way he always gives thanks. And in the way he never speaks of anyone with less than common grace. In the way he always stood for the underdog. And in the way he always tries to bring hope to fading faith. And in the way he always spoke well of the opponents who borrowed his space.

Now for the last, yet my favorite of all. In the way he smiles with his eyes. In the way he always stood tall. And in the way he outshines us all. With one glance, the angels fall.

© Howard Bingham

Dad and me at his house in Berrien Springs, Michigan.

THE FOOTPRINTS OF AN ANGEL

I have seen great trails outwalked
but never a tale so gracefully taught.
And I have stood for principles firsthand,
but never for those so dear to man
as the ones for which he stands.
Nor ever have I seen a smile
so widely flowered and endlessly enlaced
than that of the one he's embraced.
And although I have loved with all my might,
beyond all of space and sky,
never have I loved as high as his heart has managed to fly.
And never will another follow more closely
to the footprints of the angel in front of me.

UNWAVERING PRIDE

LAILA ALI

Thank you, Dad, for blazing the trail that I have continued on.

Side by side, yet on my own, I will prevail and rise to the throne that awaits me by the grace of my name.

All of its greatness I will sustain as I walk with unwavering pride, my faith will never subside.

Thank you for paving the way on this endless path that I will continue to blaze.

Wars of nations are fought to change maps. But wars of poverty are fought to map change.

—Muhammad Ali

Dad hanging out in the hotel room.

THE PLAN

Muhammad Ali

When I think of all the money I've made, I ask myself, Why should these people from the ghetto and hardworking households come pay to see my fights, making me rich and the promoters rich, and get nothing back in return? There will be more tough fights in the ring for me, but my toughest fight is still to come when I retire from boxing. That will be the continued fight to help my people.

I shall show myself to the people. I shall go out to colleges and schools and lecture. I shall go down to the slums and roam the streets, talk to the poor folks and the drunks and the bums.

I just want to make them happy.

LOOK AT ALL THE BUILDINGS

MUHAMMAD ALI

Look at all the buildings in downtown New York.
People built them.
They're dead now,
but the buildings are still standing.
We don't own anything; we're just trustees.
Think about it!
We're all going to die.
This life is a test.
Try and pass the test.
I'm trying, and I'm going to make it to heaven.
That's the eternal life.

A MESSAGE TO THE WORLD

MUHAMMAD ALI

They'll just have to look at all the records of all the fighters, look at all my actions. And then it is up to the people to rank me where they want. I can't say boxing doesn't mean anything to me. All I'm in it for is security and the livelihood of my children. When I'm through, that's it. You're going to think what you want, but the record speaks for itself.

They'll have to say that I was the fastest heavyweight that ever lived.

They'll have to say that I was the best-looking in the face, unscratched and unmarked.

They'll have to say that I was the most educated with the best diction, at colleges and as seen on TV debates, with writers and interviewers.

They'll have to say I was the only real world champion. I fought in such places as Arabia and exhibitions in such places as Peru, Venezuela, Argentina, London, Switzerland, Japan, and Israel.

They'll have to say that I was the most famous man worldwide, more famous than any other fighter in history.

They'll have to say that I invented the "rope-a-dope" and the "Ali Shuffle."

Dad and me in his office at our home in Los Angeles.

They'll have to say that I was the only prophet in the game that could predict the knockout rounds.

They'll have to say that I was the "peoples'" champ.

They'll have to say that when I stopped boxing, the game died.

They'll have to say that I was and still am the Greatest!

© Howard Bingham

Dad and me in his yard in Berrien Springs, Michigan.

Old age is just a record of one's whole life.

—MUHAMMAD ALI

Dad in a hotel room reading fan mail.

GOD'S GRAND NAME

He's witnessed mountains fall and cities rise.
He's seen passion pouring from lamenting eyes.
He's heard voices call out lonely cries,
to go unattended by common minds.

He laid down principles before all of mankind
and sewed their noble threads through time.
Then he conquered the resistance from negative vibes.

And earned his place in God's grand eye.

Despite inhuman, overwhelming tides,
he never once let virtue die.
He tied the ribbon where angels fly.

And earned his place in God's grand sky.

He claimed his victories with gracious eyes,
and loved his rivals throughout the ride,
never letting scorn inside.

He's earned his place in God's grand time.

Now as you watch his pace grow slow
or hear his soft voice flow,

do not be fooled by his slow hand,
or that swift motion which once flew grand.

Muhammad Ali will rise again,
and his sharp mind will still win the game.
Only this flame burns in heaven's domain.

Because he's earned his place, in God's grand name.

I will retire someday, perhaps soon, but I will never forsake boxing. I just hope that the people in boxing don't forsake it after I'm gone.

—MUHAMMAD ALI

PARKINSON'S

MUHAMMAD ALI

When Ali first met him,
Parkinson's was grinning.
Parkinson's scared, but he can't run
and he can't hide.
From the world's greatest champion asserting his pride.

THE SURRENDER

Hana Ali

I've decided to surrender to fate.
The clouds will lead the way.
I'm going to make the most of each given day.
I'm going to live and breathe in faith.
The stars will lie out my name.
I'm going to make the most of my time,
I have all the world's love to find,
and all of God's strength as mine.
Now I'm going to blaze a trail,
where all great hearts can prevail.
And together in heaven we'll dwell,
where love never goes unfelt
and arms never fold unhealed

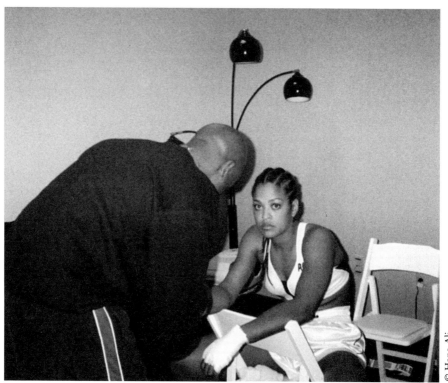

ACKNOWLEDGMENTS

I would like to thank the following people for helping make this book possible: my dad; my mother, Veronica; Lonnie; Ron D. Necola, my father's lawyer; Susan Crawford, my literary agent; Tracy Sherrod, my editor; Calaya Reid; Howard Bingham, our family friend and photographer; Tim and Helga Shannahan; everyone at Pocket Books, Simon & Schuster; my friend, Kim Richardson, for helping me get the book in by my deadline.

I would like to thank everyone who has and will support me on my life quest. Thank you all, and I hope you will enjoy reading the book as much as I have living it.

HANA ALI